CORNERSTONES OF FREEDOM™

THE TITANIC

BY PETER BENOIT

CHILDREN'S PRESS®
An Imprint of Scholastic Inc.
New York   Toronto   London   Auckland   Sydney
Mexico City   New Delhi   Hong Kong
Danbury, Connecticut

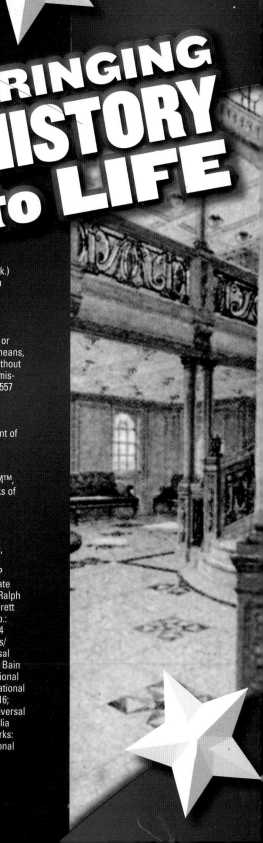

BRINGING
HISTORY
to LIFE

Content Consultant
James Marten, PhD
Professor and Chair, History Department
Marquette University
Milwaukee, Wisconsin

Library of Congress Cataloging-in-Publication Data
Benoit, Peter, 1955–
   The Titanic/by Peter Benoit.
      p. cm.—(Cornerstones of freedom)
   Audience: Grade 4 to 6.
   Includes bibliographical references and index.
   ISBN 978-0-531-23607-9 (lib. bdg.) — ISBN 978-0-531-21965-2 (pbk.)
   1. Titanic (Steamship)—Juvenile literature. 2. Shipwrecks—North
Atlantic Ocean—Juvenile literature. I. Title.
   G530.T6B559 2013
   910.9163'4—dc23   2012034325

All rights reserved. Published in 2013 by Children's Press, an imprint of
Scholastic Inc.
Printed in the United States of America 113

SCHOLASTIC, CHILDREN'S PRESS, CORNERSTONES OF FREEDOM™,
and associated logos are trademarks and/or registered trademarks of
Scholastic Inc.

1 2 3 4 5 6 7 8 9 10 R 22 21 20 19 18 17 16 15 14 13

Photographs © 2013: Alamy Images: 29 (Enno Kleinert/dieKleinert),
40 (Everett Collection Inc.), 35 (GL Archive), back cover (Lordprice
Collection), 20 (Mary Evans Picture Library), 13, 58 (UK History); AP
Images/Jim MacMillan: 48, 57 bottom; Bridgeman Art Library/Private
Collection/© Look and Learn: 30; Corbis Images: 4 bottom, 23, 51 (Ralph
White), 46 (Wang Lei/Xinhua Press); Dreamstime/Bowie15: 28; Everett
Collection/Merie Weismiller Wallace/© 20th Century Fox Film Corp.:
54; Getty Images: 50, 59 (Emory Kristof/National Geographic), 12, 44
(Hulton Archive), 55 (John Moore), 17 (Roger Viollet), 49 (Steve Liss/
Time Life Pictures), 18 (Topical Press Agency/Stringer), 10 (Universal
Images Group); Library of Congress: 7, 8, 22, 36 (George Grantham Bain
Collection), 43, 57 top (Harris & Ewing), 26 (John S. Johnston); National
Archives and Records Administration/ARC Identifier 278339: 47; National
Geographic Stock/Raymond Wong: 39; Photo Researchers: 4 top, 16;
Shutterstock, Inc./Melissa King: 5 bottom, 24; SuperStock, Inc./Universal
Images Group: 21; The Art Archive/Picture Desk/Ocean Memorabilia
Collection: 14; The Granger Collection: 6, 11, 32, 34; The Image Works:
cover, 42 (akg-images), 45 (ILN/Mary Evans), 25 (Mary Evans/National
Archives), 2, 3, 15, 27, 56 (Mary Evans/Onslow Auctions), 5 top, 37
(Syracuse Newspapers), 33 (The Print Collector/HIP).

Maps by XNR Productions, Inc.

Did you know that studying history can be fun?

BRING HISTORY TO LIFE by becoming a history investigator. Examine the evidence (primary and secondary source materials); cross-examine the people and witnesses. Take a look at what was happening at the time—but be careful! What happened years ago might suddenly become incredibly interesting and change the way you think!

Contents

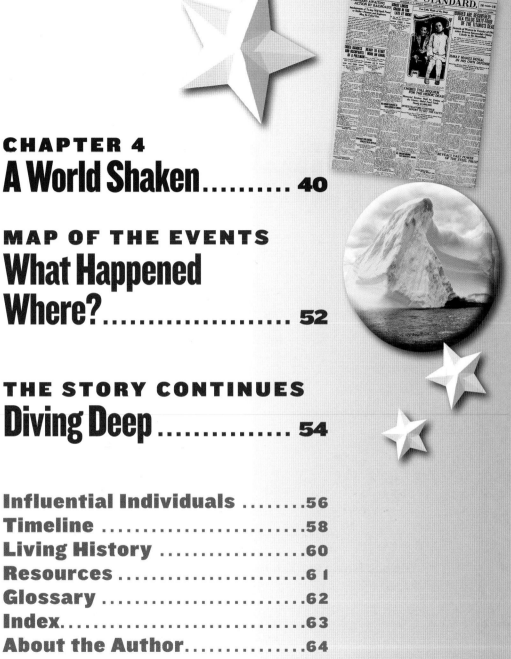

A New Kind of Ship

J. Bruce Ismay worked to improve the White Star Line's ships.

In 1899, upon the death of his father, J. Bruce Ismay took control of the family business. The White Star Line was known around the world for its passenger ships. Under Ismay's leadership, the company began to focus on more luxurious ships.

THE *TITANIC* WAS BUILT TO

The time was ripe for change. White Star's main competitor, Cunard, launched the passenger ships *Lusitania* and *Mauretania* in 1906. The ships did not provide the luxurious accommodations that many first-class passengers demanded, but they were very fast. The *Mauretania* almost immediately set a world record for the fastest trip across the Atlantic Ocean, traveling around 2,800 miles (4,500 kilometers) in four days, 10 hours, and 41 minutes. Rather than trying to challenge the speed record, Ismay decided to compete by building huge ships with world-class accommodations. The Irish shipbuilding company Harland and Wolff was charged with designing three huge new ocean liners. They would be named *Titanic*, *Olympic*, and *Britannic*. Ismay approved the designs in late July 1908. Soon, the *Titanic* would become famous around the world, though not for the reasons Ismay had hoped.

The *Lusitania* was one of the fastest ships of its time.

COMPETE WITH THE *LUSITANIA*.

CHAPTER 1

THE CROWN OF CIVILIZATION

The *Titanic* and the *Olympic* were constructed side by side.

THE CONSTRUCTION OF THE

Titanic posed challenges unlike any Harland and Wolff had experienced. The new ship was so large that it would not fit in the **slipways** where earlier ships had been built. A new double slipway was built before the *Titanic*'s **keel** could be laid down. Three hundred frames crossed the keel every 3 feet (0.9 meters) and reached to the uppermost level of the **hull**. Two thousand steel plates weighing several tons each were attached to the frames using three million steel rivets. Despite their immense size, none of these hull plates were more than 1.5 inches (3.8 centimeters) thick.

This diagram shows how the *Titanic*'s bulkheads were designed to rise above the water level.

Safety First

The designers at Harland and Wolff knew that the *Titanic* would flood with water if its keel were punctured. To protect against this, they originally planned to add a second set of steel plates 7 feet (2 m) above the lower ones. But in an effort to cut weight, this full double hull was not approved for the final design. The plans also called for 15 **bulkheads** to divide the hull into 16 sections. Each bulkhead had a watertight door that could be opened. This would allow the crew and passengers to move between the sections. The door would close automatically if more than 6 inches (15.2 cm) of water flooded the section.

The *Titanic* was designed to stay afloat even if the four sections at its **bow** were ruptured or if two central sections flooded. However, the bulkheads added weight and expense to the *Titanic*'s construction. As a result, they reached only to the saloon deck, less than 15 feet (4.6 m) above water level. The ship's designers did not believe that the six front sections could ever

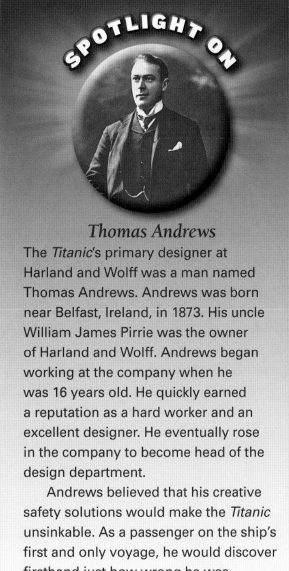

SPOTLIGHT ON

Thomas Andrews

The *Titanic*'s primary designer at Harland and Wolff was a man named Thomas Andrews. Andrews was born near Belfast, Ireland, in 1873. His uncle William James Pirrie was the owner of Harland and Wolff. Andrews began working at the company when he was 16 years old. He quickly earned a reputation as a hard worker and an excellent designer. He eventually rose in the company to become head of the design department.

Andrews believed that his creative safety solutions would make the *Titanic* unsinkable. As a passenger on the ship's first and only voyage, he would discover firsthand just how wrong he was.

be damaged at once. But they knew that if this ever occurred, rising water would eventually spill over the bulkhead separating the sixth and seventh sections. One compartment after another would flood, and the ship would surely sink.

A FIRSTHAND LOOK AT
THE *TITANIC*'S BLUEPRINTS

Blueprints drawn up by the designers at Harland and Wolff confirm the *Titanic*'s commitment to spacious luxury. They also show fatal design flaws. See page 60 for a link to look at the blueprints online.

The *Titanic* had only 20 lifeboats, with a combined capacity to carry 1,187 people. However, the ocean liner was certified to carry 3,547 passengers. This was partially because the size of ships had increased dramatically over the previous two decades. Laws only

Twenty lifeboats lined the sides of the *Titanic*.

The *Titanic* was massive compared to other ships of its time.

considered safety requirements for ships weighing around 10,000 tons. Such ships were required to carry at least 16 lifeboats. The *Titanic* was designed to be one of the largest ocean liners the world had ever seen. When completed, it weighed 46,328 tons. This was almost five times the size of the largest ships mentioned by lifeboat laws of the time.

The *Titanic* was 882 feet long (268.8 m) and 92 feet (28 m) wide, with eight **decks**. The ship had four giant smokestacks and a massive **rudder**. Its three propellers were the size of enormous windmills. They were driven

Massive engines powered the *Titanic* on its voyage.

by three huge engines. The engines were driven by steam produced in 29 immense boilers. The boilers were powered by 159 coal-burning furnaces. The *Titanic's* crew shoveled more than 600 tons of coal daily into those furnaces.

The Lap of Luxury

The 337 first-class passengers on the *Titanic's* upper decks could scarcely imagine the infernal heat of the engine rooms or the endless toil of the workers shoveling coal. Instead, they enjoyed the accommodations of an upscale hotel. The *Titanic* was home to a swimming pool, a gymnasium, a barbershop, and a library. Passengers chatted and listened to live music in a lounge decorated with green velvet and polished oak. They dined on steak, oysters, and other fine foods. Men relaxed in soft chairs beside a marble fireplace in the ship's reading room as their children played out on the deck.

The ship's 271 second-class passengers enjoyed accommodations almost as grand. They took turns playing

TODAY'S PERSPECTIVE

By 1912, White Star was locked in a battle with Cunard to offer the fastest trips across the Atlantic Ocean. Realizing that Cunard had it beat when it came to speed, White Star poured its money into building luxurious liners with world-class accommodations. However, these ships still needed to be fast because they delivered mail. As a result, speed was sometimes valued above safety. Ships often pushed forward even in dangerous conditions. The sinking of the *Titanic* served to correct this way of thinking. New safety measures were put in place. Today, experts believe that this emphasis on speed was one of the main causes of the *Titanic* disaster.

the piano in the second-class dining room, sipped coffee, and relaxed in leather chairs. In the mornings, they ate breakfasts of ham, sausage, eggs, and tea in the dining room of the saloon deck.

The *Titanic* carried 712 third-class passengers on its voyage. No other ocean liner offered such high standards for the price. Third-class passengers had access to a bar and a smoking room. Accustomed to unending work in their jobs on land, most of them enjoyed the ship's offering of music and dance. These men and women came from 20 nations around the globe. There were 43 Americans and 118 British people traveling third class. Dozens more came from Sweden, Lebanon, Finland, and Austria-Hungary.

First-class rooms were comfortable and well decorated.

Hundreds of people enjoyed the comforts of the *Titanic*.

They had boarded the *Titanic*—traveling from Southampton, England, to New York City, New York— for a variety of reasons. Some were simply looking for a good time. Others were hoping to find safety, freedom, and opportunity in a new country. They had no idea what horrors lay before them.

CHAPTER 2

"ICEBERG RIGHT AHEAD!"

The *Olympic* was launched in 1910 and its maiden voyage was in 1911.

THE *TITANIC'S* SISTER SHIP

Olympic made its first voyage in June 1911. Cheering crowds gathered when it arrived in New York. J. Bruce Ismay was one of the ship's passengers. His trip aboard the *Olympic* gave him ideas for changes to the *Titanic*. These upgrades included additional cabins and upper decks. They would make the *Titanic* even more attractive to first-class passengers.

Too large to dock at Cherbourg, France, the *Titanic* floated in the waters nearby as passengers rode to it on smaller vessels.

When passengers boarded the *Titanic* on April 10, 1912, the dangers of the northern Atlantic Ocean were far from their thoughts. The ship's operation was expected to be so smooth that passengers would forget they were traveling across an ocean.

Setting Sail

Before making the trip across the Atlantic, the *Titanic* first traveled 80 miles (129 kilometers) from Southampton, England, to Cherbourg, France, to pick up more passengers. There, the ship dropped anchor at 6:30 p.m.

The dock facilities at Cherbourg were not prepared for a ship as large as the *Titanic*. As a result, two smaller White Star ships had to ferry passengers out to the ocean liner from the shore. After the Cherbourg passengers were loaded, the ship made one more stop in Queenstown, Ireland, to pick up more passengers. Then it began its journey toward New York.

Crew members carried luggage aboard for the new passengers boarding in Queenstown.

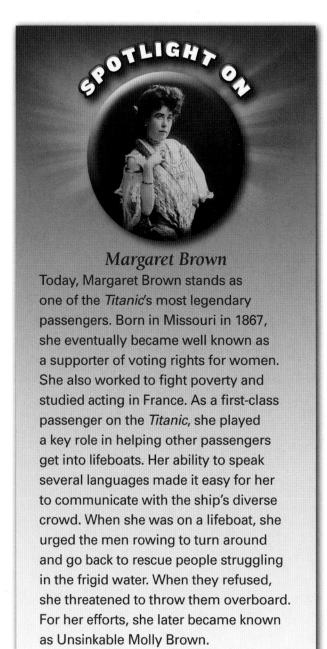

Margaret Brown

Today, Margaret Brown stands as one of the *Titanic*'s most legendary passengers. Born in Missouri in 1867, she eventually became well known as a supporter of voting rights for women. She also worked to fight poverty and studied acting in France. As a first-class passenger on the *Titanic*, she played a key role in helping other passengers get into lifeboats. Her ability to speak several languages made it easy for her to communicate with the ship's diverse crowd. When she was on a lifeboat, she urged the men rowing to turn around and go back to rescue people struggling in the frigid water. When they refused, she threatened to throw them overboard. For her efforts, she later became known as Unsinkable Molly Brown.

The ship's passenger list was packed with famous names. Among those embarking were American investor John Jacob Astor IV, political activist Margaret Brown, and fashion designer Lucy Christiana. Railroad owners John Thayer and Charles Hays were traveling with their wives. Thayer's 17-year-old son, Jack, was returning home to Pennsylvania with his parents.

Controversial British newsman and social activist W. T. Stead had booked passage after being invited by U.S. president William Howard Taft to speak at a peace conference. Isidor Straus, co-owner of Macy's department store, was on board with his beloved wife, Ida. These passengers were

Captain Edward Smith (right) and crew member Walter McElroy stand aboard the *Titanic* during its voyage from Southampton to Queenstown.

used to the finest of everything. They were impressed with the *Titanic*'s luxurious accommodations. Ismay and *Titanic* designer Thomas Andrews accompanied them on the voyage.

Before the Crash

The *Titanic*'s captain, Edward Smith, was an experienced and widely respected sailor. He was also a superb storyteller with a developed sense of hospitality that put passengers at ease. Aware of the season's potential for icebergs and storms in the northern Atlantic Ocean, he charted a route that led more southward.

Icebergs still remained a potential danger, however. All experienced seamen feared darkness. Ice could become a deadly hazard when visibility was reduced. To complicate matters, the ship's lookouts had no access to binoculars. Crew member David Blair had been assigned to a different ship before the *Titanic* had departed. He had left the ship's binoculars in a locker to which no one on board the *Titanic* had a key. The lack of such important equipment added to the difficulties the *Titanic* would soon face.

Icebergs can be dangerous obstacles for ships when visibility is low.

Jack Phillips was one of the *Titanic*'s two wireless communications operators.

In all, the *Titanic* had 892 crew members. Radio operators Jack Phillips and Harold Bride were two of the most important ones. They were employed by the wireless communication company rather than White Star, and their loyalties were divided. The communication company wanted to make sure that passengers were able to send and receive personal messages. Some of the *Titanic*'s first-class passengers used the ship's powerful wireless communications to direct business from the ocean. Others simply wanted to

La Touraine **warned the** ***Titanic***'**s crew that there would be ice ahead.**

let friends know they were on the grandest ship afloat.
But wireless communications were also used to pass
messages, including ice warnings, between ships. Such
messages were important to the ship's navigation. They
were always supposed to take priority over passengers'
messages. On Sunday, April 14, the Titanic's wireless
communication system was swamped with messages.

The ship had received its first notification of ice from
the ocean liner La Touraine two days earlier. By Sunday, the
messages had become more frequent and urgent. In all,

the *Titanic* received six ice warnings from other ships, but failed to process and forward them to the **bridge** effectively. Captain Smith received the second ice warning at 1:42 p.m. He spoke with Ismay about the issue and then set the *Titanic* on a more southerly course. He never received the third warning that came in a few minutes later. It warned that ice had also been seen to the south. On Sunday evening, urgent reports from a nearby ship, the *Californian*, confirmed sightings of large icebergs.

Captain Smith did not receive the warnings of dangerous ice promptly.

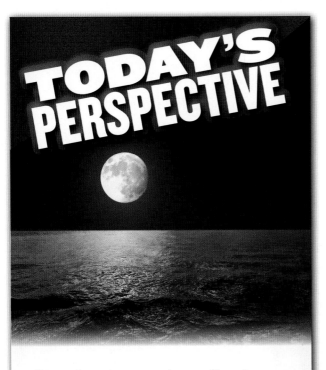

TODAY'S PERSPECTIVE

Recently, **astronomers** have offered an explanation for the unusual number of icebergs in the North Atlantic in April 1912. The sun was unusually close to Earth on January 3. The following day, the moon was closer to Earth than normal. This caused tides to rise higher than usual around the globe. Astronomers have proposed that higher tides might have lifted icebergs from the shallow water where they rested. Once in the ocean current, the icebergs drifted slowly southward and into the *Titanic*'s path. The wreck of the *Titanic* may have been written in the stars!

Jack Phillips was busy transmitting passenger messages. As a result, he failed to make sure the *Californian*'s warnings reached the bridge. The *Californian* stopped moving for the night to ensure that it did not collide with the surrounding ice. The *Titanic*'s crew was unaware of this risk, however. The ship pushed onward.

At 11:39 p.m., lookout Frederick Fleet spotted an iceberg straight ahead of the ship. Fleet promptly sounded the lookout bell and telephoned officer James Moody on the bridge to forward his observation: "Iceberg right ahead!" Moody sent the message to officer William Murdoch. Murdoch quickly ordered that the ship be

Though the ship's crew tried to avoid a collision, the *Titanic* still scraped against the side of the iceberg.

turned to the left to avoid hitting the ice head-on. The ship's center propeller was also stopped in hopes that the ship would slow down before colliding with the ice.

Below, passengers in their cabins heard a scraping sound and felt a mild jolt as the *Titanic*'s engines fell silent. In the middle of the Atlantic on a cold night, with 2 miles (3.2 km) of frigid water beneath them, the passengers clung to the crew's assurances that all would be well.

CHAPTER 3

AND THE BAND PLAYED ON

The collision with the iceberg caused massive damage to the ship's hull.

THE *TITANIC* WAS DOOMED AS much by its own construction as by human error on the night of the crash. Stopping the ship's center propeller may have slowed the *Titanic*, but it also made the rudder less effective and the ship harder to turn. Ten feet (3 m) above the keel, but several feet below the ocean surface, the *Titanic*'s **starboard** side scraped along the iceberg. Steel rivets, made brittle by icy Atlantic waters, snapped at the point of impact as the starboard hull buckled. Water immediately began pouring in.

Difficult Decisions

After the impact, Captain Smith and Thomas Andrews conducted a brief inspection of the damage. What they found alarmed them. The *Titanic*'s bow had already begun to dip downward. The ship tilted starboard as the six forward sections began to fill with water. With so many compartments ruptured, there would be no way to stop frigid Atlantic waters from pouring over the bulkheads and into other sections. Andrews knew the *Titanic* would sink quickly. Captain Smith hurried to the radio cabin and ordered wireless operators Phillips and Bride to transmit distress signals. The ship RMS *Carpathia* responded, but it was at least three hours away.

The *Carpathia* received the *Titanic*'s distress signal, but was too far away to reach the sinking ship quickly.

Members of the *Titanic*'s crew pose while wearing life jackets.

Captain Smith weighed the problems facing him and ordered the *Titanic*'s lifeboats to be readied for launch. Crew members moved quickly from cabin to cabin and alerted the sleeping passengers in first and second class to put on life jackets. They were told to make their way to the sun deck, where lifeboats would be waiting.

A FIRSTHAND LOOK AT
THE *TITANIC'S* SOS MESSAGES

After the *Titanic* struck the iceberg, its crew members sent out messages requesting help. They stated that the ship was "sinking fast" and gave the location where they could be found. See page 60 for a link to view a record of one of these messages online.

Lifeboats were slowly lowered into the icy water below.

Women and Children First

Captain Smith charged William Murdoch with loading starboard lifeboats and Charles Lightoller with loading those on the **port** side. He also gave orders that women and children were to be the first ones on the lifeboats.

Around an hour after the collision, lifeboat 7 was the first to be lowered over the *Titanic*'s starboard side. Though it could fit 65 occupants, only around 25 were aboard. Passengers reasonably feared being lowered eight stories from a sinking ship past rushing waters. Around the same time, 24 passengers, including Margaret Brown, boarded lifeboat 6 on the port side. Officer Joseph Boxhall launched distress signals from the starboard bridge in an effort to alert the *Californian*.

Once in the water, lifeboat passengers rowed to get away from the sinking *Titanic*.

These signals only alarmed the growing number of passengers on deck. Remaining passengers began to doubt the comforting words that the *Titanic*'s crew had offered them earlier. Twelve people boarded starboard lifeboat 1, which had a capacity of 40.

John Jacob Astor died in the sinking of the *Titanic*, though he was able to get his pregnant wife safely aboard a lifeboat.

Women boarded lifeboats with their small children, while their husbands and older children were barred from leaving. Ida and Isidor Straus, married for 40 years, refused to get on lifeboats when it meant they would be separated. Sixteen-year-old Alfred Gaskell twice tried to board lifeboat 14 and was removed at gunpoint. However, the lifeboat launched with 25 empty spaces. John Jacob Astor coaxed his pregnant wife into lifeboat 4, but did not resist when Lightoller barred him from joining her. Ismay did not follow the "women and children first" policy. He stepped into a lifeboat and was able to escape the sinking ship.

YESTERDAY'S HEADLINES

J. Bruce Ismay survived the sinking of the *Titanic*, but his life was never the same. His decision to abandon the sinking ship earned him a reputation as a coward in the United States. He was mercilessly ridiculed in the press, especially in newspapers owned by William Randolph Hearst. Hearst's newspapers ran a full-page cartoon titled "This is J. Brute Ismay." The cartoon depicted Ismay watching the *Titanic* sink from the safety of his lifeboat.

A VIEW FROM ABROAD

After the disaster, news spread about the heroic efforts of Wallace Hartley and the *Titanic* band. None of the band members had survived. People across Great Britain were amazed and saddened by the tale of the musicians' sacrifice. As a result, the recovery of Wallace Hartley's body generated widespread interest. Packed in ice, Hartley's remains were returned to his hometown of Colne, East Lancashire, England. On May 24, 1912, several orchestras performed together at London's Royal Albert Hall to pay tribute to Wallace Hartley and the *Titanic* band. In all, almost 500 musicians played at the concert.

The Final Moments

As the lifeboats departed, disorder began to break out on deck. The *Titanic*'s bandleader, Wallace Hartley, directed his musicians to continue playing in an effort to calm the doomed passengers. The band played on as the waters of the Atlantic swirled about them. Finally, shortly after 2:00 a.m., the last lifeboat was launched. Some desperate passengers prepared to jump as the *Titanic* disintegrated under the strain of overwhelming forces.

The ship began to tilt at a steeper angle. The lights went out, and the hull split in two. The ship's sturdy keel barely held the two parts of the broken hull together.

The ship's **stern** rose quickly as its bow continued to fill with water. Survivors in lifeboats feared that the plunging ship's suction would sink them if they turned back. As a result, they did not dare rush to the aid of others. At about 2:20 a.m., the upright stern disappeared under the waves. A terrible noise filled the air as hundreds of doomed men and women struggled to survive in the frigid ocean water. Over the course of the next hour, most lost this struggle. Survivors sat stunned and shivering in their lifeboats as they waited for help to arrive.

The *Titanic* began sinking toward the ocean floor as the ship split in half.

CHAPTER 4

A WORLD SHAKEN

This photo of a waiting *Titanic* lifeboat was taken from the *Carpathia* as it approached the site of the tragedy.

REMARKABLY, THE CARPATHIA'S wireless operator had missed the *Titanic*'s first distress calls. When he finally learned of the ship's situation, he immediately alerted the *Carpathia*'s captain, Arthur Rostron. The *Carpathia* set off toward the sinking *Titanic* right away. Survivors saw the *Carpathia*'s lights appear on the horizon a little more than an hour later. After another hour, the ship finally arrived among the waiting lifeboats. In total darkness, its crew began to rescue the survivors from their boats.

Once they were safely aboard the *Carpathia*, the *Titanic*'s survivors warmed themselves and struggled to deal with the tragedy they had just experienced.

Rescue Efforts

Some of the survivors were strong enough to climb aboard the *Carpathia* using rope ladders. Others were too severely injured or exhausted to climb the ladders. They were raised up using slings. Terrified children were lifted up in mail sacks. Once aboard the ship, the dazed and quiet survivors received medical attention.

Daybreak revealed a world of ice. Large icebergs seemed to be everywhere. One was streaked with red paint at its waterline, presumably from a collision with the *Titanic*. As the *Carpathia*'s crew was completing its rescue work, the *Californian* arrived. Captain Rostron requested that the *Californian* continue to search for survivors in the surrounding waters. He then turned the *Carpathia* toward New York. He and his crew had managed to save 705 survivors.

Reactions Around the World

By 2:00 a.m., disturbing rumors of the *Titanic*'s sinking had already reached New York. Earlier, a Canadian wireless station had received alerts of the unfolding catastrophe. About the same time, the cargo vessel the *Virginian* received the *Titanic*'s distress message and reported it to officers on land

TODAY'S PERSPECTIVE

At the *Titanic* inquiries, Frederick Fleet (above) and his fellow lookout George Symons testified about a hazy horizon. That haze is only now being fully grasped. The unusual amount of North Atlantic ice in April 1912 cooled the air at the ocean's surface, bending light rays downward. Cold air **mirages** can result in false horizons, making it hard to see what is really in the distance. The *Californian* may have misinterpreted the *Titanic*'s distress signals because of mirage conditions. The signals seemed unusually close to the horizon and did not give the appearance that the great liner was sinking. Today, scientists have suggested that the unusual appearance of the *Titanic*'s distress rockets may have been the result of a cold water mirage, which may also have concealed the iceberg from the ship's lookouts.

in Montreal, Quebec. The officers forwarded this news to local newspapers. The newspapers contacted the *New York Times* to help spread the information.

People who heard the news could not believe that such a thing had happened. One transmission reported incorrectly that the *Titanic* was being towed to Halifax, Nova Scotia. Many found hope in this report. But the horrible reality of the *Titanic*'s final hours began to emerge on both sides of the Atlantic by 6:00 p.m. on April 16. More than 1,500 people had died in the frigid waters of the Atlantic. In Belfast, Ireland, the shipbuilders at Harland and Wolff were devastated. Having built the *Titanic* themselves, they couldn't help

Newspapers around the world reported on the *Titanic*'s sinking as the number of dead continued to rise.

THE BRIEF CAREER OF THE LARGEST LINER
DESCRIBED IN THREE TABLEAUX

—THE LEVIATHAN (AND HER COMMANDER, CAPTAIN SMITH) LEAVING SOUTHAMPTON—

APRIL 10

DEPARTURE

The *Mackay-Bennett* recovered hundreds of bodies from the site of the *Titanic*'s sinking.

but feel partly responsible. As news of the event spread, all the world mourned the *Titanic*'s loss. Hopeful relatives of missing passengers lined up at White Star's offices, more often than not leaving in tears.

Searching for the Truth

White Star hired the *Mackay-Bennett* out of Halifax, Nova Scotia, to search for bodies at the site of the sinking. The ship sailed on April 17. It carried hundreds of coffins

TODAY'S PERSPECTIVE

On April 17, 1912, the mostly volunteer crew of the *Mackay-Bennett* pulled the body of a little boy from the Atlantic Ocean. He appeared to be no more than two years old, and the crew was unable to determine his identity. Heartbroken by the death of such a young child, the ship's men paid for his burial in the Fairview Cemetery of Halifax, Nova Scotia.

In 2007, almost 100 years after the boy's body was discovered, scientists performed **DNA** tests on samples from the teeth and bones. Thanks to these tests, they were able to identify him as Sidney Leslie Goodwin (above). The *Titanic*'s unknown child at last had a name.

and several tons of ice. When it arrived at the scene of the disaster, its crew found hundreds of corpses in white life jackets bobbing in the ocean. The *Mackay-Bennett* recovered 306 bodies. Three other ships also searched for corpses and found fewer bodies.

As the *Mackay-Bennett* sailed off on its grim mission, U.S. senator William Alden Smith agreed to head a congressional investigation of the *Titanic*'s sinking. The investigators hoped to discover the exact causes of the disaster. Questioning of the crew began on April 19 in New York City and was later moved to Washington, D.C. Many of the *Titanic*'s British crew members complained that they were being unfairly prevented from returning home.

Great Britain's Board of Trade soon began its own investigation. The two investigations agreed on many facts. The *Titanic* had been going too fast. The ship had not been equipped with enough lifeboats, and those lifeboats had not been loaded efficiently. Also, the *Californian* had not responded to distress signals as quickly as it should have.

Some historians believe that more people would have survived the *Titanic* disaster if the *Californian* had responded faster.

Dr. Robert Ballard led the search for the *Titanic*'s wreckage in the 1980s.

After the investigations, many new laws were put in place to protect ships and their passengers in the future. One of these laws required ships to carry enough lifeboats for all passengers aboard. Another required all crew members to undergo training in lifeboat usage. Bulkheads would in the future have to be extended far above the waterline. This would make the individual sections of ships totally watertight. Finally, an International Ice Patrol was established to track icebergs in the northern Atlantic Ocean.

Diving into the Past

The *Titanic*'s sinking dominated news coverage in the weeks following the disaster. Its two sections had plummeted 12,500 feet (3,810 m) before coming to rest on the bottom of the Atlantic. As time passed, the *Titanic*'s incredible story continued to occupy imaginations. Though never far from people's thoughts, the ship's remains would not be seen again for 73 years.

In the 1980s, advances in deep-sea exploration began to fuel interest in locating the wreck. **Oceanographer** Robert Ballard had developed an undersea video camera sled called *Argo*. Hoping to use this new device to explore the *Titanic*, Ballard secured funding from the U.S. Navy to search the floor of the Atlantic.

Crowds gather to watch as Dr. Ballard and his team return from an expedition to the *Titanic* wreckage.

Using *Argo*, Ballard found the *Titanic*'s remains on September 1, 1985. The ocean liner lay in two large sections on the ocean floor, with smaller pieces strewn about. The next summer, Ballard's team returned to the wreck with a manned **submersible** named *Alvin*. They traveled to the ocean floor and photographed the pieces of the ship. Popular interest in the *Titanic* exploded as a result of Ballard's work. Many *Titanic* expeditions have now been undertaken. Submersibles with mechanical arms and sampling baskets have recovered thousands of artifacts. These artifacts have helped historians understand many important details of the *Titanic*'s story.

This photo of the *Titanic*'s bow was taken by a submersible.

Journeys to the *Titanic* wreckage have turned up a variety of artifacts, including plates, clothing, and tools.

Critics of the expeditions point out that frequent visits to the site have caused the *Titanic* to begin falling apart at a faster rate. In addition, ocean life-forms have eaten the ship's wood and worn away at its hull. In recent years, investigators have raced to make a detailed map of the wreck and its surroundings before it is lost forever.

A FIRSTHAND LOOK AT
BALLARD'S EXPEDITION

Robert Ballard and his crew documented their search for the *Titanic* with extensive photography and a large amount of video footage. See page 60 for a link to watch some of this video footage online.

What Happened Where?

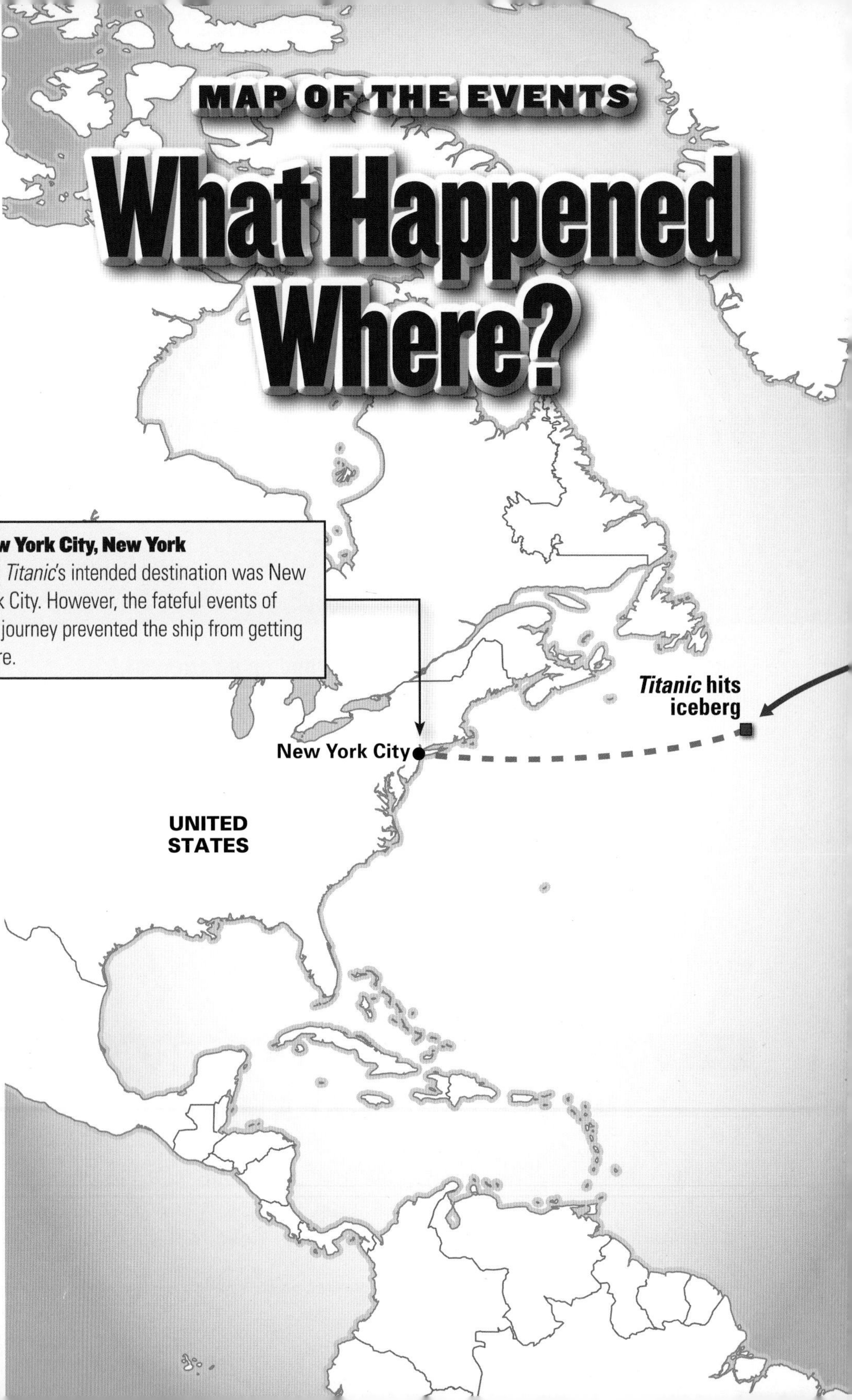

New York City, New York

The *Titanic*'s intended destination was New York City. However, the fateful events of the journey prevented the ship from getting there.

***Titanic* hits iceberg**

New York City●

UNITED STATES

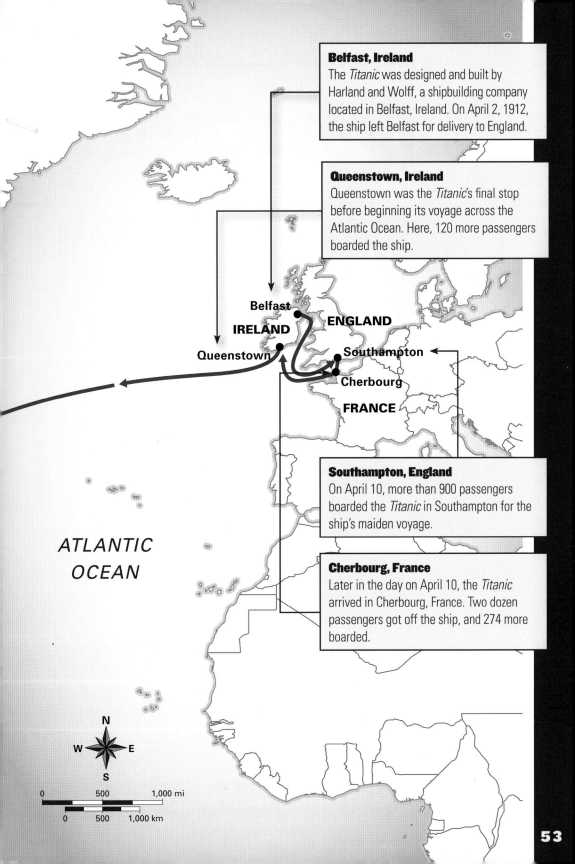

Belfast, Ireland
The *Titanic* was designed and built by Harland and Wolff, a shipbuilding company located in Belfast, Ireland. On April 2, 1912, the ship left Belfast for delivery to England.

Queenstown, Ireland
Queenstown was the *Titanic*'s final stop before beginning its voyage across the Atlantic Ocean. Here, 120 more passengers boarded the ship.

Southampton, England
On April 10, more than 900 passengers boarded the *Titanic* in Southampton for the ship's maiden voyage.

Cherbourg, France
Later in the day on April 10, the *Titanic* arrived in Cherbourg, France. Two dozen passengers got off the ship, and 274 more boarded.

Belfast

IRELAND

ENGLAND

Queenstown

Southampton

Cherbourg

FRANCE

ATLANTIC
OCEAN

N
W · E
S

0	500	1,000 mi

0	500	1,000 km

Diving Deep

The 1997 film *Titanic* inspired many people to take a renewed interest in the ship's history.

Lives were changed forever on that fateful night in mid-April 1912. More than 1,500 people died, while many others survived to carry on the *Titanic*'s story. The last survivor of the disaster died in 2009, but the ship's legacy will live forever.

In 1912, the *Titanic*'s sinking challenged people's belief in the power of technological progress. The disaster showed that even humankind's biggest, most advanced creations could fail. Even the world's greatest shipbuilders could make mistakes.

Since the sinking, the *Titanic* and its passengers have remained constant subjects of the public's imagination. Movies, books, and even video games have all been based on the ship's incredible history. The *Titanic* may have sunk more than 100 years ago, but its story will not be forgotten anytime soon.

Museum exhibits around the world give people a chance to get an up close look at *Titanic* artifacts.

TWO BILLION DOLLARS AT THE BOX OFFICE.

INFLUENTIAL INDIVIDUALS

Edward Smith

Edward Smith (1850–1912) was the captain of the *Titanic*. Many people later questioned his decisions during the night the ship sank.

William Alden Smith (1859–1932) was the U.S. senator who led the investigation into the sinking of the *Titanic*. He was portrayed negatively in the British press for his handling of the investigation.

J. Bruce Ismay (1862–1937) was the manager of the White Star Line. He chose to escape the sinking *Titanic* on a lifeboat even though many other passengers were unable to do so. As a result, he earned a reputation as a coward.

Margaret Brown (1867–1932) was a supporter of childhood education and women's voting rights who was among the *Titanic*'s passengers. For her efforts in helping to load the ship's lifeboats, she later became known as the Unsinkable Molly Brown.

Arthur Rostron (1869–1940) was the captain of the *Carpathia*, the ship that first came to the aid of survivors in the *Titanic*'s lifeboats.

Thomas Andrews (1873–1912) was the *Titanic*'s main designer. He played a central role in decisions regarding the ship's layout and construction. As a result, he may have been the first person on the *Titanic* to understand that the ship was doomed.

Wallace Hartley (1878–1912) was a violinist who served as the leader of the *Titanic*'s band. He and his fellow band members sacrificed their lives to soothe the ship's doomed passengers.

Frederick Fleet

Frederick Fleet (1887–1965) was the *Titanic*'s lookout who first saw the iceberg that the ship would soon hit. He survived the sinking but suffered greatly from guilt. He hanged himself in 1965.

Robert D. Ballard (1942–) is an oceanographer and underwater archaeologist. He is best known for his 1985 discovery of the wrecked *Titanic*.

Robert D. Ballard

TIMELINE

1906

Cunard launches the *Lusitania* and the *Mauretania*.

1908

J. Bruce Ismay approves Thomas Andrews's designs for the *Titanic*.

April 15, 1912

12:05 a.m.
Captain Smith orders the *Titanic*'s lifeboats to be uncovered.

12:45–2:05 a.m.
One by one, lifeboats are loaded and launched.

2:17 a.m.
The *Titanic*'s keel breaks, the bow sinks, and the stern rises to a vertical position.

2:20–4:10 a.m.
The *Titanic*'s surviving passengers and crew wait for rescue in frigid ocean water.

4:10 a.m.
The *Carpathia* arrives to rescue survivors from lifeboats.

1912

April 10
The *Titanic* sets sail from Southampton, England.

April 12
The *Titanic* receives warnings of nearby icebergs from the ocean liner *La Touraine*.

April 14
The *Titanic* receives numerous ice warnings from other ships.

April 14, 1912

11:39 p.m.
The *Titanic*'s lookout Frederick Fleet spots an iceberg straight ahead.

11:40 p.m.
The *Titanic* collides with the iceberg.

1912 continued

April 17
The ship *Mackay-Bennett* begins recovering bodies from the site of the sinking.

April 18
The *Carpathia* docks in New York, carrying the *Titanic*'s survivors.

April 19
William Alden Smith begins the U.S. Senate investigation into the *Titanic*'s sinking.

May 18
The *Titanic* bandleader Wallace Hartley is buried in Colne, East Lancashire, England.

1985

Oceanographer Robert D. Ballard discovers the *Titanic*'s wreckage on the floor of the Atlantic Ocean.

LIVING HISTORY

Primary sources provide firsthand evidence about a topic. Witnesses to a historical event create primary sources. They include autobiographies, newspaper reports of the time, oral histories, photographs, and memoirs. A secondary source analyzes primary sources, and is one step or more removed from the event. Secondary sources include textbooks, encyclopedias, and commentaries. To view the following primary and secondary sources, go to www.factsfornow.scholastic.com. Enter the keyword **Titanic** and look for the Living History logo ∑¦.

∑¦ **Ballard's Expedition** Robert Ballard's trip to the floor of the Atlantic Ocean to discover the *Titanic*'s wreckage marked the first time in 73 years that anyone had seen the *Titanic*. Ballard and his crew preserved the expedition through photographs and video footage, much of which can be viewed online.

∑¦ **The *Titanic*'s Blueprints** Harland and Wolff's blueprints for the *Titanic* show off the ship's incredible size and luxurious accommodations. Today, we can also look at them to see just where the company went wrong in designing the ship's safety systems.

∑¦ **The *Titanic*'s Passenger List** It was once common for newspapers to publish lists of passengers on large ocean liners such as the *Titanic* and its sister ships. As a result, an almost complete record of the *Titanic*'s passengers still exists today.

∑¦ **The *Titanic*'s SOS Messages** As the *Titanic* sank, its crew members sent out SOS messages in hopes that a nearby ship would come to their aid before it was too late. An original record of one of these messages can be viewed online.

RESOURCES

Books

Adams, Simon. *Titanic*. New York: DK Children, 2009.

Brewster, Hugh, and Laurie Coulter. *882½ Amazing Answers to Your Questions About the Titanic*. New York: Scholastic Paperbacks, 2012.

DK Publishing. *Story of the Titanic*. New York: DK Children, 2012.

Pipe, Jim. *Titanic*. Richmond Hill, ON: Firefly Books, 2007.

Visit this Scholastic Web site for more information on the *Titanic*:
www.factsfornow.scholastic.com
Enter the keyword Titanic

GLOSSARY

astronomers (uh-STRAH-nuh-murz) scientists who study planets, stars, and space

bow (BOU) the front section of a ship or boat

bridge (BRIJ) the part of a ship from which it is navigated and piloted

bulkheads (BUHLK-hedz) walls built within the hull of a ship in order to reduce the risk of flooding

decks (DEKS) different levels of a ship

DNA (DEE EN AY) short for deoxyribonucleic acid, the molecule that carries genes, found inside the nucleus of cells

hull (HUHL) the frame or body of a boat or ship

keel (KEEL) the structure along the bottom of a boat or ship that keeps it stable and upright

mirages (muh-RAHZH-iz) things people see that are not really there, especially water

oceanographer (oh-shuh-NAH-gruh-fur) a scientist who studies the ocean and the plants and animals that live in it

port (PORT) the left side of a ship as one faces forward

rudder (RUHD-ur) a hinged piece of wood or metal attached to the back of a boat, ship, or airplane and used for steering

slipways (SLIP-wayz) ramps built on the shore that allow boats to be moved in and out of water

starboard (STAHR-burd) the right side of a ship as one faces forward

stern (STURN) the rear end of a ship or boat

submersible (suhb-MUR-suh-bul) a small underwater vehicle

Page numbers in *italics* indicate illustrations.

ABOUT THE AUTHOR

Peter Benoit is a graduate of Skidmore College in Saratoga Springs, New York. His degree is in mathematics. He is the author of dozens of Children's Press books, with topics as diverse as Native Americans, ecosystems, disasters, American history, and ancient civilizations.